Freedom For No One

Thoughts on Non-Duality

D. Justine Jeyaraj & Andreas Müller

Impressum

Bibliografische Information der Deutschen Nationalbibliothek: Die Deutsche Nationalbibliothek verzeichnet diese Publikation in der Deutschen Nationalbibliografie; detaillierte bibliografische Daten sind im Internet über www.dnb.de abrufbar.

Covergestaltung: Andreas Müller

Verlag:
BoD · Books on Demand GmbH, In de Tarpen 42,
22848 Norderstedt
Druck:
Libri Plureos GmbH, Friedensallee 273, 22763 Hamburg

ISBN: 978-3-7693-1072-6

Content

D. JUSTINE JEYARAJ

D. Justine Jeyaraj was born in 1951 into a Catholic Christian family at Tiruchirappalli, Tamilnadu, India. Graduate in B.A.Sociology.

"I entered into Government of India service as Stenographer, with M/s Bharat Heavy Electricals Limited, Tiruchirappalli.

For two years after joining duty, I lived a normal young man's life of music, movies and friends.

In 1972, suddenly I found life was not as it seemed to be. I became acutely aware of the suffering of Humanity.

I first read the book, 'Thought Power' of Swami Sivananda of Rishikesh, Himalayas, India. Then I had a meeting with Fr. Bede Griffiths, of Shantivanam, Kulittalai, Tamilnadu, India. His meeting promised me safety in spiritual life. In the mean time, I devoured thousands of spiritual books available on this earth. But I was growing more and more panic stricken.

And I found a great spiritual asylum in a magnificent Guru Sri La Sri Pandrimalai Swamikal. He initiated me into a powerful Mantra towards worshipping god Murugan, the Deity of Tamilians.

It was a successful pursuit that benefited me with material and spiritual benefits, along with rare siddhies, psychic powers like telepathy, precognition, and healing powers. I was happily married to my wife Bella. We were blessed with a rare and highly gifted girl child, who is now a Dentist abroad.

I got spiritual ENLIGHTENMENT on 30-4-1984. I resigned my lucrative government job, which was a shock to many. But my wife who also worked for the Government took it all cool and supported and sustained me.

For few years I managed to live my Enlightened state, though all along I felt it to be a limitation. I started feeling uncomfortable in it.

On 19-2-2007, by 12-15 pm I stumbled upon the website Actual Freedom of Richard. Then I never turned back. I became actually free in 3 years."

But soon I found that Actual Freedom too was not real freedom because there was still a PERSON in me, who was trying to enjoy freedom. And that freedom was elusive. I remained still bound and suffered anxiety and restlessness. I suffered this agony for more than a decade.

One day in late 2022, while scrolling in my iPad, I came across a website called thetimelesswonder.com., created by a young man called Andreas Muller. Whatever I read in that website gave me literally goose bumps. I knew that at last I have arrived at something I longed for more than 50 years, as I'm now in my seventies."

The fundamental message of Andreas was just this:

"THERE IS NO ONE".

It was a shock to me!

It didn't take much time. May be a month or two.

I just died. But I did not do that either. That's what apparently happened. For no one.

I realized "Who cares for freedom or no freedom?".

I got in touch with Andreas by E-mails almost for the whole year of 2023.

I asked questions. And Andreas always answered them with loving concern.

What transpired between Justine and Andreas correspondences is verbatim reported in this book called "FREEDOM FOR NO ONE".

Good Luck and prosperity for all who read this book!

E-mail: jkoperumcholan@gmail.com

Andreas Müller

Andreas was born in 1979 in Ludwigsburg in Southern Germany.
After years of seeking in spirituality, he met Tony Parsons in 2009.
"First, I was shocked. Though I had already known and experienced
a lot, this was something new and unexpected. Suddenly, for no
reason, I heard what Tony was saying, and soon it was undeniable:
There is no one."
Since 2011, Andreas has been holding talks and intensives
throughout the world.

www.thetimelesswonder.com

You reading these lines does not have to make sense. In fact, it cannot make sense. Reading these lines is all there is. THAT IS IT. THAT IS WHOLENESS. So what should it make sense for? It simply cannot because there is nothing else it could make sense for. Nothing in this book has meaning. YOU READING THESE LINES IS NO-THING. THAT IS 'IT'.

- ANDREAS

The following conversations were made via e-mail
thoughout the year 2023.

It was due to D Justine Jeyaraj's initiative that this book was
happening.

Justine & Andreas
No. 1

Justine:	*What do you teach?*
Andreas:	Nothing. It's all perfect already. So, there is nothing to teach.
Justine:	*How can I see that?*
Andreas:	Well, you will never really see that. You refer to an additional state of seeing. Perfection can't and doesn't have to be seen. It just is.
Justine*:*	*There is no truth?*
Andreas:	No, there isn't. There isn't a real happening in the first place, so, yes, there is no truth.
Justine:	*What happened to you then?*
Andreas:	Nothing happened to me. I just died. But I did not do that either. That's what apparently happened, again for no one.
Justine:	*'What is' doesn't recognize itself?*
Andreas:	No, it doesn't. 'What is' doesn't recognize itself to be something. It just is what it is, without any need for recognition.
Justine:	*Does it know itself?*
Andreas:	Not really. It just is itself. You know (laughs), 'sitting In this room' just is perfectly itself – there is no real knowing of any kind in that. It

just is what it is. No one knows what it is, no one knows how it is and no one even knows if something is at all.

Justine: *Is there a 'me' now or not?*

Andreas: No, of course not. It's not there.

Justine: *Is 'what is' real or unreal?*

Andreas: There is no such thing as "what is". That's why I say 'no-thing'. 'What is' even isn't an 'it'. Try to know 'no-thing' and it will not work. It doesn't say anything.

Justine: *What is it?*

Andreas: There is not anything. There is no one there to know. This – what seems to be happening - is timelessly no-thing. It is naturally whole and complete. However, there is no experiencer of 'what seems to be happening'.

Justine: *When I hear you speak about there not being any experience, this sounds rather dead and boring.*

Andreas: It's empty but not dead. In fact, it's pretty alive. Yet there is no one experiencing anything, and there isn't some-thing that's experienced. Insofar, the end of experiencing doesn't look attractive to the 'I'. 'Me' doesn't want to die.

Justine:	*Why are there no answers?*
Andreas:	There is no answer, because there is no real happening in the first place.
Justine:	*How can you say there's no happening?*
Andreas:	That's the answer that comes out. I died. Answers seem to come out of that apparent death.
Justine:	*Is there something like absolute awareness?*
Andreas:	No, there isn't something like absolute awareness, but there is no-thing as apparent awareness.
Justine:	*What about all these spiritual paths and teachings?*
Andreas:	They all refer to a person, which doesn't exist, in order to heal a separation that isn't there either.
Justine:	*Ramana said, "Be what you are". What do you think?*
Andreas:	Well, the question is who should do that, who needs to do that? There is no one. You can't "do" being who you are. You already are what you are.
Justine:	*Do you never get stressed?*

Andreas:	I do get stressed - apparently, effortlessly, of course.
Justine:	*Nisargadatta Maharaj suggested staying in the 'I am'.*
Andreas:	It's not working. There is no one. 'I am' is an illusion. To stay in the 'I am', to go beyond the 'I am', is just futile.
Justine:	*Who am I? Can't I 'self-enquire'?*
Andreas:	No. Who wants to inquire? Who wants to come to conclusions and know? There is no one. It's all the 'me', which has no reality at all.

***

Justine:	*With my death it's all over?*
Andreas:	Well, yes and no. Nothing can be known really. Who would know whether something ends or whether something goes on?
Justine:	*It's better to stop seeking?*
Andreas:	Who could do so? There is no one there. There is no seeker in seeking, and there is no finder in liberation.
Justine:	*Have you reached "Perfect liberation"?*
Andreas:	All there is, is perfect liberation. But 'you' can't

have it. When "perfect liberation" happens, nothing happens. It never went away, so you can't gain it. Liberation is not personal. It's not a state. It's not even an 'it'. All there is is this apparent happening, which is natural, simple and perfectly itself.

Justine: *Wow, it's really simple - but also very intense.*

Andreas: Yes, it's very simple. It simply is. And yes, seen from the apparent perspective of 'me', it's intense.

Justine: *So, is it always that intense?*

Andreas: Well, it's total, but also empty. It's totally itself, however, it's free from reality and meaning.

***

Justine: *Do you think that we have to resolve issues?*

Andreas: No, I don't think so. However, it's not about the issues. There just is no one who needs to do so. Leave the issues alone, or leave yourself alone, and everything will take care of itself.

Justine: *What if there are any traumas or heavy stuff going on?*

Andreas: Then that's what apparently happens. Seen by the 'me', the whole existence is an unresolved issue. Which can't be answered at all. Same with traumas too.

Justine: *Can this be life changing?*

Andreas: Yes, of course. Falling off of traumas may change the behaviour of the apparent body. Everything just seems to level out a bit. For no one of course.

Justine: *And when there are still traumas left over time?*

Andreas: Then that's what apparently happens. Look, this whole thing doesn't contain any real value. Being traumatized is as much wholeness as anything else. The whole idea - and the experience - of being someone who is on a path is nothing but a dream. Healing - or no healing - is what apparently happens. Life apparently happens. It already is free. As it is. As you are. As I am. Even if there seems to be an Andreas who wants this or that, there is no person behind it.
The person is an illusion. It doesn't exist.

Justine: *Oh, wow, that's wonderful.*

Andreas: Yes, it is. For no one.

***

Justine: *I am getting older and chances to realize seem to get less and less. What shall I do with that?*

Andreas:	Well. I don't know. The main thing is that there is no one.
Justine:	*What's it's worth if I can't experience perfection?*
Andreas:	Oh, nothing. It's not worth anything. It's not something that you own and can use. It simply is what you are.
Justine:	*To me, it all seems very difficult.*
Andreas:	Yes, that's true. The 'I' is struggling with this. It's impossible to do because, it already is whole and complete. All experience is illusory. 'What is' is naturally whole already, no matter what it looks like or what it feels like. Everything is totally and absolutely well in being what it is. Pain, feelings, don't complain themselves. Someone experiences pain and suffering. He lives in the illusion of suffering from pain, instead of there being just pain. Fortunately, there is no one.
Justine:	*Is suffering an illusion then?*
Andreas:	Well, pain is what apparently happens, but yes, the sufferer is illusory. No one suffers from anything. But feelings that the 'me' would regard as suffering may apparently happen.

***

Justine:	*How can I see that I am not real?*
Andreas:	Not at all. You can neither comprehend nor see that, just because there's no 'you'. Who will be able to do that? There is no one.
Justine:	*But I can't see it.*
Andreas:	Yes, simply because there is nothing to see. That's it. Nothing has been found. Nothing has been additionally seen. It's just the end of the illusion of there being a seeker.

***

Justine:	*Is this message for everyone?*
Andreas:	Theoretically it's for everyone. Practically, it's only for those who are interested in it. Only few are interested, compared to people who are drawn to spiritual offers. Also many lose interest soon. They don't get what they are looking for. They don't get highs of spiritual uplifting.

***

Justine:	*How can the seeker end itself?*
Andreas:	The seeker can't end itself, because there isn't even a seeker. The seeker doesn't exist.
Justine:	*How can I make this become obvious?*

Andreas: You can't. I can't. Nobody can. Everybody is just helpless here. There is no way out and no way in. There is no path, because everything is already the goal.

***

JUSTINE'S NOTES
ON ANDREAS

Andreas:	There is nothing to find. There is no one seeking, because there is no one alive.
Justine:	*Without knowing this, I wandered like a dog for 40 years after gurus. I found no peace, but only more troubles.*

***

Andreas:	The unknown. No-thing appearing as it appears. It is already whole. It is already complete. IT IS READING THESE LINES. It is you.
Justine:	*So far, no one has said this. I experience INSTANT PEACE in this.*

***

Andreas:	You reading these lines does not have to make sense. In fact, it cannot make sense. Reading these lines is all there is. THAT IS IT. THAT IS WHOLENESS. So what should it make sense for? It simply cannot because there is nothing else it could make sense for. Nothing in this book has meaning. YOU READING THESE LINES IS NO-THING. THAT IS 'IT'.
Justine:	*Reading this, I FLOAT IN THE SEVENTH HEAVEN!*

***

Andreas:	I have not found what I was looking for. I was looking for love, for peace, for ecstasy, for relief, for bliss - and I failed. And while I kept on seeking, for what I

thought would bring fulfilment, I VANISHED. While I vanished, it became obvious that there is no one vanishing. While I vanished, it turned out that I WAS NEVER THERE in the first place.

Justine: *None of the gurus I met never said this. They all taught me that one day I will become like God, one with God. What an impossible chimera! What a delusion they taught me to pursue tirelessly. My condition almost ended in a state of PTSD.*

***

Andreas: There is no way to realise oneness because all there is, is oneness. It already is realised. The dilemma in all this is you. But in fact, AS YOU DO NOT EXIST, there is no dilemma either.

Justine: *What a heaven...Cool cool...everything heavenly!*

***

Andreas: God is absolutely blind. That is why she sees no differences. She is not looking anywhere. There is no fairness in it. The only fairness is that all of existence is just God herself. Whatever you decided, whatever you fucked up, and whatever you succeeded in, IT IS ALL THAT. Neither of those is real. Neither of those has a separate existence and holds any meaning. It is free energy, wildly performing its magnificent dance.

Justine: *This perspective is grand.*

Andreas: Reality is already NO-THING and NON-DUAL. It does not have to and can not be reached by you, in fact, as long as you apparently are, you will live in the dream of separation. So, YOU WILL NEVER GET IT. You will never become liberated. YET, YOU ARE LIBERATION.

Justine: *Now it's clear why all my toils for sense of freedom never happened.*

***

Andreas: If the dropping of 'me' happens, it's an energetic "event". It is something that happens with you! And not within your experience. It does not happen to the personality, to your ego or to your body. No, it happens with your sense of being! With your apparent innermost being. With the 'thing' that experiences itself as alive...WITH YOU.

Justine: *Here, I get clear definition of my ego, the personality and how the dropping of the 'me' happens.*

***

Andreas: 'Me' lives in a subtle sense of "the best is yet to come". It's a dream. Nothing will come. There is no future. THIS DOES NOT HAVE A NEXT MOMENT. Reading these lines is 'it'. There is nothing else. This is the best. It already is.

Justine: *Tra la la la la ...! I want to sing out of joy.*

***

Andreas: Liberation really happens for no one, meaning that you will not survive. Though it may sound a little bit tragic, it is actually not that bad. Because, when it happens, it turns out that 'YOU NEVER EXISTED'. So, there is nothing to worry about.

Justine: *Spiritual teachers never go this deep to explain the existential facts. Gurus mostly talk about rewards and punishments, karma, this world and other worlds, higher beings and subtle dimensions that never give peace or quiet to the seeker.*

***

Andreas: Liberation is death. It is total relaxation. It is not 'YOU' that is relaxing. No one dies because no one lives. Death is not a moment of death - it is timeless. Liberation is not a moment of liberation - it is timeless.

Justine: *All teachings, religions, and spirituality focus on the person, the 'you'. They put you in endless pain, despair and hopelessness. It is really pathetic.*
            Andreas message is actually an eye opener. In the beginning it seems very dry, tasteless and lacking comfort. When properly understood it brings a great release of utter brilliance and peace. Even euphoria, delight and exhilaration.

***

Andreas: While the apparent me apparently rushes around to seek some-thing - liberation, wisdom, bliss, love, silence - IT OVERLOOKS THAT ALL THERE IS IS NO-THING.

Justine: *No teacher comes forward to teach 'NO-THING' because no one will come to buy nothing.*

***

Andreas: God's beauty, the beauty of NO-THING, is raw, cruel and ruthless as well as graceful and smooth. It does not know 'right' or 'wrong' nor does it give meaning to 'pleasant or 'unpleasant'. Without an act of embracing everything is timelessly embraced - BY NO ONE.

Justine: *An EMPTY FULLNESS FOR NO ONE*

***

Andreas: All religions, all philosophy, spirituality, health, gurus, family or financial advisors are based on the assumption that there is SOMEONE - A REAL PERSON who is separate from life. Yet, there is not any one. There is no such thing as a life that exists in time and space. A phantom, an illusion wants to navigate through an illusory life.

Justine: *No wonder what an agony that 'non existing*

person' experiences in that 'non existing life'.
Suffering seems to be illusory. But for the
suffering person, it is real and cruel too.

***

Andreas: There is no one. There is no real heaven and there is
            no real hell - there is just the UNKNOWN appearing
            as that. However, this does not make hell less
            painful. The apparent pain of hell is as much
            wholeness and aliveness as the apparent joy of
            heaven. It is not dead, it is pretty alive , for it is being
            aliveness itself. THAT IS FREEDOM.

Justine: *For humans there is more hell than heaven.*

***

Andreas: It is good - as it is! It is wholeness already, which is
            beyond any idea of 'bad'. Good and bad, in that
            sense, do not exist - they are part of the dream of 'I
            am'. What is left without 'me' is WHOLENESS
            WITHOUT ANYONE PERCEIVING IT.

Justine: *Well said. Entire humanity is not aware of this fact.*
            Religions and politics have enhanced wars and
            disputes. God or Existence is Peace itself. But for
            human beings peace is an impossible thing here. The
            'me' predominates each individual and the result is
            this war ridden earth. No one can fathom this
            mystery.

***

Andreas:	When 'me' dies, no one dies. 'Me' Never existed, and never did doer-ship and choice never existed. There is no absolution because no one ever sinned. Life takes and kills you when it wants to. Whether you want it or not, does not matter. No one asks you. Why at all? YOU DO NOT EXIST.
Justine:	*Oh my God! It never occurred to me. Andreas has got it well.*

***

Andreas:	How could anything that does not exist find real FULFILMENT? How can anything that does not exist ARRIVE somewhere, at a place THAT DOES NOT EXIST?
Justine:	*How? NEVER. NEVER.*

***

Andreas:	What to do? Nothing. Who could do or not do anything? There is no one.
Justine:	*Scary!*

***

Andreas:	There is no need for anything to happen. This is just for nothing. Isn't that wonderful? It's already whole and complete, utterly vibrant and vibrantly alive.

Justine:	*YES INDEED!*

***

Andreas:	'What is' - which is all there is - does not need any realisation. In fact, it cannot be realised because it is already realised. 'What appears' is the absolute realisation of God. No-thing mappearing as this, just is. It is very simple.
Justine:	*It is as simple as that. Why these teachers confused us, threatened us?*

***

Andreas:	As beingness shines everywhere, nothing has to be known or felt or perceived.
Justine:	*Oh! What a peace!!*

***

Andreas:	You do not have to be peaceful in order to be 'this'. 'What is' does not need any prerequisites in order to be 'what is'. That is the great FREEDOM, which does not belong to anyone.
Justine:	*This is really GREAT!*

***

Andreas:	There is no path, no method and no knowledge that

can take you 'out here'. There is nothing that will lead you to a real, more enlightened state. There is nothing that can make WHOLENESS MORE WHOLE.

Justine: *Yes. It's for sure.*

***

Andreas: All there is, is what is. There is sitting or lying, holding a book, reading, thoughts happen, body sensations, feelings, a room or the sky. That is what appears. That is all.

Justine: *Nothing more? Angels, psychic powers, fate, destiny, karma, disease? Nothing?*

***

Andreas: What appears, appears without reason and without sense. What appears does not come from anywhere nor does it go anywhere. It has no past, no present and no future. It simply is without meaning and without intention. What appears, appears outside of time and outside of space. It simply is. WONDERFULLY SIMPLE AND YET COMPLETELY ABSOLUTE.

Justine: *Enough, enough, enough...joy, joy, joy!*

***

Andreas: That which appears is NOTHING. Nothing in particular. Not this or that. One could not call it some-thing, but NO-THING. It only is what appears. No second, no next! NEITHER 'I' NOR 'YOU' NOR 'GOD' NOR ANYTHING ELSE. This perspective remains hidden for the apparent 'Me'.

Justine: *And the whole HELL BROKE OUT!*

***

Andreas: There is nothing being aware of 'what is', there is just 'what Is'.

Justine: *Mind boggling.*

***

Andreas: A 'near-death' experience is NO-THING appearing as that. It is within the story. In fact, no one dies, because no one is alive.

Justine: *Ha..Ha..!*

***

Andreas: Love is all there is. However, love is NO-THING. It is having this conversation, looking at each other and so on. This is love appearing as that.

Justine: *That's all...ha ..ha...!*

***

Andreas: Oneness does not need anything to be oneness.

That is its freedom. It is this. That which appears. The room, chairs, you, me, the conversation. That is oneness. Oneness is not a thing. People, chairs, you and me are not things. That is the dream: that there are lots of separate things going on. But there are not things. So, oneness is not many. And it is not one either. IT IS NO-THING.

Justine: *Oh, my God! My breath stops!*

***

Andreas: There is no one there to be liberated. There is no one there to be ANYTHING.

Justine: *This is enough to be happy.. I celebrate!*

***

Andreas: Some sort of wisdom may appear, but for sure no one is having it. Liberation is the end of the person. Fortunately, this does not require wisdom.

Justine: *Hi jolly jolly!*

***

Andreas: There is nothing real. Sitting, breathing, talking, this room. This is NO-THING. That's all.

Justine: *Unbelievable. But it is so!*

***

Andreas:	This is the miracle. This is the unknown - sitting, breathing, talking. That's it. When you die, there is no one looking any more. What is left then, is no-thing. What is left is this. What is left is the unknown.
Justine:	*Tasteless. But soothing to hear!*

***

Andreas:	'Me' will never recognise oneness. No one does. When me' dies, what is left is oneness without anyone recognising it.
Justine:	*Mind boggling, again!*

***

Andreas:	Who is Andreas? He is illusory, and doesn't count much.
Justine:	*This point - Andreas says in a world where traditionally teachers and gurus demanded worship and veneration from their devotees. Hats off to you, Andreas!*

***

Andreas:	Andreas is NO-THING appearing as Andreas.
Justine:	*Gurus never had the humility to say this. Shame to them!*

***

Andreas: There is nothing to remind you of. Certainly not your true nature - there is not any.

Justine: *The world of spiritual teachers abound with teachings reminding one's true nature.*

***

Andreas: There is Just what apparently happens - whatever that is. It can be silence as well as turmoil. Both are 'it'.

Justine: *Religions ascribe silence to the divine and turmoil to the devil.*

***

Andreas: There is no Message. That is the message: THERE IS NONE. All there is, is this. NO-THING. There still seems to be Andreas, a table, a room. That's the miracle: that nothing changes. Nothing has to change, nothing can change - because NOTHING EXISTS.

Justine: *Mind boggling, again!*

***

Andreas: I'm not. I'm not real. Andreas is not a thing that exists. He never did actually. May be, if we become friends one day, you will be really disappointed because I am merely ordinary - not very enlightened. I'm not more or less special than you are. Actually I'm not at all. NO ONE IS, BUT HARDLY ANYONE CLAIMS IT.

Justine: *True humility.*

***

Andreas: Truth cannot be spoken, because there is no truth. All there is, is this. NO-THING appearing as you and me having this conversation.

Justine: *Okay.*

***

Andreas: Neither clarity nor confusion matter. I mean, who cares?

Justine: *Yes.*

***

Andreas: 'I' already doesn't exist. The sense of 'I am' simply is what appears. No one is doing it. That is all there is: sitting here, having this conversation, That's it. Nothing else exists. There are no entities here.

Justine: *A blessed state.*

***

Andreas:	I don't see anyone. I don't see a person sitting in front of me. I'm not even looking. There is no one alive, so there is no one looking.
Justine:	*I can understand.This is true freedom! This is true freedom!!*

***

Andreas:	Liberation is happiness. But that's not for anyone. There is no entity that is happy.
Justine:	*Andreas, you are really liberated man!*

***

Andreas:	Liberation is bliss, but there is no experience of bliss. Feelings of bliss may appear but they don't mean anything.
Justine:	*Okay.*

***

Andreas:	For the apparent me NO-THING might look boring, because it expects something. For me it's boring. No-thing is not imaginable. May be the 'Me' tries to imagine nothing. And yes, that may appear to be boring because it is looking it FROM THE OUTSIDE. 'Me' looks from itself as the centre into space and sees chairs, people, this room and says slightly sceptical: "Oh, that's all there is...? That's the

ultimate truth...? - Yes, That's all there is.

Justine: *An extraordinary statement.*

***

Andreas: There is no such thing as Peace. There is no world either.

Justine: *Mind boggling.*

***

Andreas: War in Ukraine is sad. Yet it's Wholeness. It's not real in the sense the apparent me thinks it is. None of these are real - neither the war nor me nor the sadness. What is real is no-thing appearing as us having this conversation. That is what appears. That's the unknown appearing as this. And that's what is!

Justine: *Very difficult to understand this. But with deep reflection what Andreas says becomes clear. Great!*

***

Andreas: What is 'what is'? This: the unknown appearing as this. That's all. Nothing else is. You ask how I find peace then? There is no YOU to find peace, and there is no peace to be found. All you may apparently find are states or experiences of something from which you think that it's peace or something close to peace.

Justine: *Sounds very complicated. But... Andreas seems correct.*

***

Andreas: a) There is no one playing the game. There is no game at all. All there is is this: No-thing appearing as these talks. That is it. THAT IS WHOLENESS.

b) Wholeness appears as a person that apparently lives in an apparent dream reality. But: There is no person, and there is no dream reality.
c) It's like 'me' sitting in emptiness. That's usually unpleasant.

d) Nothing is there any more, but you. You seek a way out. But there's nowhere to go. No other place, no next moment, no next situation coming, only in the dream of 'I am'. IT IS VERY UNPLEASANT FOR THE 'ME' TO REMAIN IN EMPTINESS.

e) This is NO-THING appearing as that.

f) This is oneness too. Yet, that is the dream. YOU ARE THE DREAM.

Justine: *Breathtaking!*

***

Andreas:	1) The belief that you are is the dream, the belief that you can do or not do anything is dream. None of this is real. So, don't care. Or do care. I don't know.
	2) Nothing dies. That's the miracle: that there isn't anything alive . THERE JUST ISN'T ANYTHING.
	3) There is not anyone. There never was anyone.
	4) There is neither an 'I' nor a soul. It is all story including time. THERE IS NO NEXT - NEITHER A NEXT MOMENT NOR A NEXT LIFE - NEITHER AN 'IN FIVE SECONDS' NOR AN 'IN TEN LIVES'.
	5) No one lives, no one dies and no one can be born again. The whole experience of being separately alive is illusory. So is reincarnation, birth and death. What remains is aliveness itself - which is unknown. What remains is no-thing WHICH IS NOT AN EXPERIENCE, and therefore unknown.
	6) The awareness thing may be pleasant. In fact, it's not really pleasant. It's cooling down the intensity of daily life, the emotions and all that stuff. Yet no one stays there.
	7) It's not even 'it'. It's no- thing.
Justine:	*Emphatic words that relieve me from tremendous burdens.*

***

Andreas: 1) The awareness gurus teach you to remain in hell.

2) I can't give you anything nor do you need anything from me. There is neither you nor me.

3) No matter how you appear, behave, feel, it is what appears. And this is Wholeness. AND: THERE IS NO ONE.

4) I don't talk. NO-THING appears as this talking, as a person called Andreas. However, there is no sense of being Andreas. Andreas Just is what seems to happen, as well as you do, chairs, room, and this conversation apparently do. That's all there is.

5) Seeking is still seeking - it is unpleasant. Yet, it is not real.

6) If you don't go to work, you will starve. Of course, you already don't go to work. Actually, you never did go to work. It's oneness that goes to work. It's oneness that sets the alarm and it's oneness that goes to the fridge and fetches a yoghurt. It's a dream that you are doing that.

7) Everything leaves, nothing remains.

8) Andreas is played out, but there is no one in the role.

9) Andreas being stressed out about coming too late to an event is life, is NO-THING appearing as that. It feels as it feels, yet, FOR NO ONE.

10) Oneness is not an experience. It is the end of you experiencing.

11) There is no self to find.

Justine: *Andreas words give TOTAL CLARITY. One may not need to read any more book or follow any teacher. He is final resort.*

***

Andreas: 1) Nothing needs to happen. Nothing can happen because nothing really happens. All happening is illusory and is no-thing.

2) There is no real dream and there is no one to leave it.

3) This message has no intention - It's not for you in order to become something else. It's not for the 'aha'. That's the difference between this and a teaching.

4) This message has a strong impact. Yet, it does not come out of an intention. It arises out of the apparent meeting between 'me' and no-thing.

5) You can't take a step to absence because there already isn't anyone. Your mere presence is illusory.

Justine:	*This message had a VERY STRONG impact on me.*

***

Andreas:	Nothing to get, nothing to understand, nothing to transcend, nothing to heal. It is this! That's the miracle, the freedom and the beauty.
Justine:	*Will anyone like this?*

***

Andreas:	1) Liberation is the end of sufferer, but not necessarily the end of suffering. For no one, of course. In that sense, the end of sufferer is also the end of suffering.

2) It doesn't have to be grasped, it can't be grasped.

3) There is nothing to find, simply because there isn't. Neither outside nor inside. You would be surprised about the simplicity of it. Because it is this.

4) It is never over, because it never began.

Justine:	*Not many can take this.*

***

Justine:	*As soon as separation drops away, is there something aware of the completeness of that?*
Andreas:	1) No. There is no awareness of anything. There is just this, which is unknown. Nothing aware of that completeness because there is not anything separate.

2) Liberation is not about the 'Me' stops working - it is the end of 'me' itself. 'Me' was never real, and therefore never did anything.

3) No one is running 'me'. Yet, as long as 'me-ing' happens, 'me' will live like this.

4) As long as 'me' happens, everything happens for 'me'. My peace, my joy, my ego, my disbelief, my success, my failure, my thoughts, my anger, my behaviour, my situation, my experience. That's the dream. IT'S SWEET AND ARROGANT.

5) NO-THING can't be experienced. No- thing is not an experience. It is 'what is', including the set up of 'I am' and experience.

6) 'I am that'. I never understood that. One could say that I am no-thing. One more great truth (laughter). When 'Me' dies what is left is 'life', but as long as there is someone, there is an experience of it. Then life is not no-thing, not the unknown, it is something.

7) In my story, there was a time with a lot of

suffering in the seeking. But I can't say that there was more 'me' or less 'me' when the suffering became less. THERE NEVER WAS ANYONE.

8) It already is everything. There is nothing else. This conversation too, is for nothing.

9) We are talking about a lot of things that are not real: HUNGER, ME, TIME.

Justine: *These things are easy to digest.*

***

Andreas: It is real and unreal.

Justine: *Can anyone understand if said like this?*

***

Andreas: 1) The whole set up of 'I am', awareness, experience, unfulfilment and seeking is illusory. It's as real and unreal as anything else. Sitting on a chair happens. Well, it apparently happens. No one is doing it. No one needs to do it. Same with everything else: breathing, thinking, feeling, the room, the atmosphere. It's all apparently happening.

2) Apparent sitting on apparent chairs in an apparent room is happening. Apparently. There is NO-THING happening. Yet, actually, no-thing is

beyond 'happening'. It is ungraspable.

3) But all there is, is no-thing. It is missing something, apparently. However, it's not real. But, yes, in the dream of 'I am' there is a sense of lack. That's part of the dream of 'I am'. When somebody says "All there is, is this", the 'me' can't see this. It can't.

4) Nothing is wrong with seeking. What it can't accept is that this whole set up is illusory. THERE IS NOTHING EXPERIENCING ANYTHING. That's the dream. That's the set up of separation. There is no experiencer, there is neither an experience nor an experienced. There is no 'I', and there is nothing experienced.

5) In liberation, what remains, sitting, breathing, is not separate, and it's REAL AND UNREAL. It's the unreal that makes it whole. And joyful, magical, fabulous.

6) Nothing is real. There is nothing real to find, but that's what the seeker wants. He wants to find something real. Something that he can rely on, something that he can have, understand, feel, work on, be proud of, show around, BUT THERE IS NOTHING REAL. It can't even find itself. How could it? - there is no one. Seeking is not real - IT IS NO-THING APPEARING AS SEEKING. It doesn't need the finding. IT'S WHOLENESS ALREADY. But NOT FOR YOU.

| Justine: | *Well said. Great clarity opens with these facts.* |

***

| Andreas: | 1) The 'I am separate' can burst INSTANTLY. It doesn't require anything - it can be like a finger snap, and the whole game is over. It's over without you becoming clearer, happier or more anything. |

2) Liberation does not happen for you. IT IS THE END OF YOU. Fear may arise. It's forever. What is left is no-thing. When the dying is over, what arises is some kind of lightness. I assumed liberation to be extra-special event. It's still amazing that it is not. It is this. Just this.

3) You don't have to do anything to be always there. I am not 'there' -'I am not', is better. And of course, I don't have to do anything for that. THERE IS NOT ANYONE WHO COULD DO SO.

4) There is nothing to be delayed or speeded up. All there is is Wholeness. It's an idea that there is more Wholeness after the apparent me isn't there any more. Yet, that idea, too, is Wholeness.

5) The desire for the whole can become very existential, while others may not even notice it. For me the seeking seemed to be so strong that it filled my whole life. I could not do normal job or get my studies done. It was not willed by me. I would not have chosen it.

6) The belief that I will get something from anything

is a dream. There isn't any real situation and there isn't anyone experiencing it.

7) All the apparent me believes to have found doesn't bring fulfilment. IT TURNS OUT TO BE NOTHING.

8) Where we can go with understanding. What happens is no-thing? All there is, is no-thing appearing as this. That's all. There is no more or anything else.

9) Who is experiencing this freedom? No one, of course. IT'S ALL FOR NOTHING.

Justine: *It's all for nothing! Ha..ha…!*

***

Andreas: 1) The apparent 'Me' thinks that something out of these talks will happen for itself. That's how it lives. IT DOESN'T LIVE BECAUSE IT IS NOT REAL. It's like a chair and the floor - an appearance. There is no instance called 'me' that has a life. In the dream of me, 'me' has a life. THAT'S THE DREAM.

2) This centre - I am - is illusory. IT'S NO-THING ITSELF APPEARING AS THE SENSE OF A CENTRE. It's not real at all.

3) This conversation itself does not only point to 'NO-THING', it is no-thing. The pointing itself is illusory and of no importance. It is for nothing.

There isn't anything which this could be good or beneficial for. THAT'S THE FREEDOM. It's already whole. This apparent conversation is already 'it'.

4) What happens is no-thing appearing as a room in which people seem to sit and talk about no-thing. That's everything. Is the everything all of that or is the everything the nothing? It's both. SITTING IN A ROOM IS NOTHING AND EVERYTHING , WHICH IS NO-THING.

5) All that appears is no-thing. The conversation we were having at breakfast was no-thing as a conversation. There was no path to it. There was no World War II, there are no Germans. What apparently happened was no-thing appearing as people sitting around a table, talking about politics in the 20th century. Sitting around a table, talking and sharing opinions is life. NONE OF THIS IS REAL, of course.

6) The appearance of 'me' is also no-thing. It's not separate. There is no real entity of a 'Me'. Yet, within its experience, it's totally clear - and the whole reality - that I was sitting at the table and that we were talking about politics and that there was a real World War II. THAT'S THE DREAM.

7) What about suffering? Is there still suffering when there is no one? Oh, yes! suffering may appear. But if there is someone, suffering is experienced as something separate and therefore as REAL. WITHOUT 'ME', IT'S NO-THING APPEARING

AS SUFFERING. And this is Wholeness.

8) Suffering as well as the avoidance of suffering - simply are life appearing as that. IN LIBERATION THERE IS NO ONE IN THEM. Life is just happening. It's like this - without any effort. There is no one who could choose. The person who wants to avoid suffering is unreal. It is not a real entity that can choose what appears. That's the illusion: That 'I' somehow play a role in this. And if 'I' knew properly, 'I' would be able to never feel pain, but feel good all the time. I don't know anyone who made it.

9) What about suicide? There is no one to choose that. In fact, there already is no one alive. Suicide is an idea in the story of 'me', an attempt to stay in control. "If everything becomes that horrible, at least I could kill myself." No, you can't. Who is there to do so? Then we only can wait. That's the next idea of the apparent me. Who is there to wait? Liberation won't come. Nothing will ever come. This is all there is. This is oneness, exactly as it is. There is no way out. For that which only lives in trying to find a way out this is tough.

Justine: *As 'me', we feel trapped. It feels uncomfortable.*

***

Andreas: 1) This - what apparently happens - is complete, absolutely complete. The apparent me assumes that tomorrow it may be more complete, namely when it becomes enlightened. This whole thing is the dream: There is no tomorrow, no next week, no next moment, no 'in five minutes'. THERE IS JUST THIS. May be there are thoughts about next week or about 'in five minutes' but that's what is apparently happening. NO-THING APPEARING AS THOUGHTS about next week. This is oneness. Oneness appearing as sitting here and thinking   about next week. THAT'S WHOLENESS and THAT'S THE JOY.

2) 'Me' labels things that don't even exist. Within the experience of 'me', there is a REAL room happening, but there isn't. There is no real room. There is no real and separate room. That is the dream 'I am' apparently lives in. It's a dream, simply because THERE ARE NO THINGS. There is neither a real world nor a real life, Including the 'me'. It has to fail.

3) Perception is dream. With death of the perceiver, perception ends.

4) WHAT REMAINS? - NOTHING. There is nothing to realise, nothing to do and nothing not to do. There is no message.

5) You cannot sum it up and get it all together, simply because there is nothing separate.

6) NO-THING appears as this. THAT IS IT.

7) Nothing to be understood. Nothing to be realised. Nothing to be approached. It already is 'IT'.

8) It already is whole - amazingly, as it is.

9) THAT IS THE MIRACLE, THE FREEDOM AND THE BEAUTY.

Justine: *PEACE, PEACE, PEACE.*

***

Justine: *In the Bible we come across Jesus getting tempted by Satan. Do such things happen in your life? If so, how do you manage? As Jesus did or in your own way? Jesus said: "Get away Satan".*

Andreas: No, when the sense of being something turns out to be inexistent, there's no challenge any more. Actually, it turns out that there never was a challenge.

***

Justine: *Are you aware you are talking a 'great message' that goes mostly unnoticed in this spiritually blinded world?*

Andreas: No, not really.

Justine: *At this young age you talk a 'brilliant message' with a global audience, thanks to modern technology. Can we say, it's Grace that works?*

Andreas: Well, it just is what seems to be happening - for no deeper reason or cause.

Justine:	*You are busy working with different levels of seekers in your intensives. I think they can torture you enough with their absurd questions. At the end of each day how do you regain your composure and go to sleep, to meet the next day?*
Andreas:	There is energy drain coming from that. I am not working with people as I am not a Guru or a coach. These answers happen effortlessly and they are impersonal and undirected.
Justine:	*Are you aware of some aid from beings from other dimensions in your almost apostolic function as a 'message giver' to the suffering people?*
Andreas:	Oh no, not at all. What we talk about here is so simple and plain. It does not need dimensions

***

Justine:	*Are you really not scared by the cruel situation of this 'real time' world situation? If so, how?*
Andreas:	There may be concerns, but there is no existential fear. There is no existence.
Justine:	*Being young, don't you think living for many more years will be boring and tiresome?*
Andreas:	No, not at all. There is no one who is having a life.

Snippets

There is no one.
There is neither someone in hell
nor is there someone in heaven.

~

You are whole and complete,
but without having an experience of being it.

~

'What happens' is not something that is.
It is no-thing for no one.

~

The natural reality is innocence.
Everything just innocently is what it is.

~

Seen by the 'me', which is permanently striving for an advantage,
this message is absolutely useless.

~

There is no experience of you being that.
'You are that', means without an
additional experience of 'I am that'.

The assumption that you're happening right now, that's the dream.
There is no happening at all.

~

Separation doesn't happen.
Experiencing doesn't happen.
There is no creation,
and there is no illusion of creation.

~

Who suffers thoughts, who enjoys silence?
There is no one.
Awareness and all these states don't exist.
Empty fullness for no one.

~

It is this experience to be a self which is aware of itself
which has no substance. This self - "I am" - is illusory.

~

The one who wants to escape from the illusion is an illusion.
Enlightenment, liberation, death of me – they all do not exist.

~

Trying to wake up is whirling around in an artificial reality. There is
neither someone asleep nor can there be a waking up.

There is no experience in deep sleep. Liberation is when there is no experiencing during day time as well.

~

That which has the experience to become awake is without any reality. When this illusion collapses, deep sleep, dream state, and day consciousness melt into no-thing.

~

This is it. There is no one. Spirituality is an illusion.

~

Trying to kill the 'me', or waking up from the 'me', fails. There is no 'me' in the first place.

~

When there is no person, there is neither someone imprisoned by what happens nor is there someone to be freed from what happens.

~

The ease is that what we speak about is already the case. 'What is' is naturally whole by simply being itself. 'What is' is absolutely at ease being what it is. What seems to be happening is naturally whole, and does not need artificial or extra state of peace or well-being.

'What is' is naturally whole, and doesn't need any experience of itself as anything to be whole.

~

Everything being whole and complete is the natural reality. It is nothing else than what seems to go on being exactly itself. Thoughts are thoughts, trees are trees and bodies are bodies. There is nothing else. It's simple and plain and obvious.

This apparent happening here and now is the uncaused, timeless, no-thing. It's whole and free already.

~

There is no escape from the body and daily life, and find a higher state to just be and rest. There are no states. That's dream: 'I experience something', or 'me and my life'.

~

No chair, no room, no thought, not even the body, experiences itself to be separate. Only self-awareness lives in the illusion of separation.

~

There is nowhere to go, no step to take. There is nowhere to be and no place to rest at. This first position - "I am" - does not happen.

It's whole already. Being me, being you, this room, my life, your life, my problems, your problems, every thought, every action, is what apparently happens.

~

There is no creation. There is no real happening in time and space. Nothing ever becomes something.

~

There is neither an 'I', nor an illusion.
It simply is, as it is - for no one.

~

The sense of presence is the sense of reality. When that turns out to be unreal, the whole impression of reality collapses.

***

JUSTINE & ANDREAS
No. 2

Q1: *Before your meeting with Tony Parsons, you had met with a spiritual guru and did sadhana for ten years. What made you come out of spirituality altogether and how?*

A1: I did several things in the ten years before I met Tony. For most of the time (approx. 5 years) I was with a guru. He was coming from Osho and Gangaji. Well, for some (no) reason I had a glimpse – an apparent moment when there was no one. From that moment on the energetic Guru-disciple dynamic was crumbling.

Q2: *For Andreas 'Whole and complete', is it an experience or No experience, ceasing of experiences? Is there an experiencer or no experiencer?*

A2: There is no experiencer.

Q3: *Can you share in detail, about your drug experiences?*

A3: That's too much to share now - it is more than 20 years ago and it feels like a past life.

Q4: *Do you still take drugs?*

A4: No, I don't, except alcohol.

Q5: In India, only drug allowed is alcohol. Can it be a substitute for the drug Ecstasy or MDMA? Can I get the same insights you had with MDMA through alcohol? Of course, I came out of spirituality through alcohol. Fortunately, I didn't become alcoholic. Can you suggest any other easily available, legal home products to use as a drug for me?

A5: I do not suggest any drug use. They have nothing to do with the apparent wholeness of everything.

Q6: After your death, are you still affected by ego, as sudden anger or depression?

A6: Well, apparently there is a character Andreas which seems to have an ego/conditioning. And yes, as it belongs to the body, it apparently affects the body.

Q7: Do you have psychic experiences? Do you get precognitive dreams or visions?

A7: No, I don't.

Q8: People like false promises. You never give any promise. Andreas talks no teacher, no teaching, his is useless talk etc. People like me, know what you talk is genuine and spontaneous. You have a family to support. Are you not worried about your precarious position? Do you believe in *destiny or divine intervention?*

A8: No, I am not scared. However, it is a miracle that I still make it financially. I don't believe in anything really.

Q9: *From where do your words originate instantly, spontaneously, without using your intellect?*

A9: They don't originate from anywhere. They are what seems to be happening and seem to come out of there not being anyone. An innocent report.

Q10: *After your ego death, what makes you sustain in a body?*

A10: Nothing. A body that sustains itself just is what seems to be happening.

Q11: *There's an old Zen koan about two monks, washing their bowls in the creek, who see two birds fighting over a frog, tearing it apart. One monk asks the other, "Why does it have to be like this?" And the other monk replies, "It's all for your benefit." What is your view on Cruelty in 'What is', Andreas?*

A11: To be honest, I don't have a view on cruelty. It is what seems to be happening, however, in all its apparent depth, there is no answer to it. In that sense, it stands for itself.

Q12: *In my spiritual days I used to silently repeat some Mantra. Now can I repeat the sentence 'There is no one'? Or is it better I ask myself, 'Who is there even to repeat this mantra - 'There is no one'.?*

A12: There is no one Justine.

Q13: *Do you watch Netflix movies?*
a) I don't, b) I have no time, c) I am not interested, d) sometimes, e) that's boring, f) Interesting indeed.

A13: Something between a) and d).

Q14: *In this video, Helsinki 2018, in first five minutes introductory talk, you give the gist of your whole talk. But you say: 'It can understand it in every talk, but also that can never be understood in a way; that it's understood that there is nothing to understand.*
It's not like an understanding in the sense of, "Now I understood it, and I won't ask a question any more in my whole life, because it's useless." No. Even that understanding Is never real'.
Wherein to rest then? Just keep floating adrift? Or....whatever....An understanding without understanding?

Is this similar to Karl Renz saying: 'Wherever you land, you have to depart again'. How to take it in the everyday practical life? A no man's land? Bizarre...? Is it   delightful for you. or you too have ups and downs, mood swings, ...sudden panic...disoriented...or   concrete   stability? You look contented and simply relaxed....no anxiety... 24x7 ZERO EXPERIENCE...? Asleep while wide awake?

A14:   Oh yes, there is no place to rest. Everything is floatingly and timelessly itself. The one who wants to find rest somewhere (= land) is illusory.
The one who wants to bring it in practical life, is illusory.
There are all kinds of mood swings, feelings, thoughts - they are floatingly and timelessly themselves. No answer, no escape, no indulgence. Already!

Q15)   *I am psychically very sensitive. It gives me lot of pain and discomfort. I want to get out of this hell. How?*

A15)   What to say Justine?! That's it.

Q16)   *I understand that this wonderful photograph was taken by you. Are you amateur or trained?*

A16)   Just an amateur.

Q17)   Do Andreas in daily life, still has any moments of annoyance? If so, how does he manage it please?

A17)   Oh yes, I do. However, no dealing with them.

Q18)   Your English is simply superb, though you are German. What is your academic qualification, sir?

A18)   I finished gymnasium is Germany and started to go to university. However, after half a year I quit and never went back.

Q19)   What all odd jobs you were engaged in finding your career life? If not interested, say pass.

A19)   That's a good question ... ... I was working in old people homes, as a fork lift driver, as courier driver, as a security, as a driver for a clinic, as a helper in a spiritual centre ...

Q20)   From your book: NO-THING UNGRASPABLE FREEDOM:
"What remains? - Nothing. There is nothing to realise, nothing to do and nothing not to do. There is no message. You cannot sum it up and get it all together. You cannot get it all together, simply because, there is nothing separate. All that is already is 'that' which you long for. All that is already is undivided - is not twoness. There is nothing to take away, nothing to take with you. As I promised in the beginning, you have not gained anything. Not because of your inadequacy, no: simply because there is

nothing to gain. Bottom line: that which is. No- thing appears as this. That is it. That Is all there is. Nothing to be understood. Nothing to be realised. Nothing to be approached. It already is 'it'. It already is whole — amazingly, as it is. That is the miracle, the freedom and the beauty." From where and how does this 'horrible world condition' comes, in the above mentioned NEAT BASE? - Justine's wrong seeing?

A20) I guess that there is no answer to this question. The horrible world situation is what seems to be happening - there is no answer to it. Nothing that explains it or that can make it acceptable. It is itself.

Q21) *Am I not coming closer to oneness?*

A21) No, you aren't. All there is, is oneness. You can't. Experiencing oneself is the dream. Experiencing a self is the dream. When 'you' die, experience also dies. What remains is 'NO - THING', which is not an experience, and therefore unknown.

Q22) *Do you smoke?*

A22) I quit 18 years ago.

Q23) *Sorry, what are we doing here?*

A23)   Nothing. No I, no we, no doing ...

Q24)   *I am growing mad that I should take the message of Andreas to as many people as possible. Especially to my ascetic daughter who I feel deserves to get this. I don't know whether she will take it or laugh at it. You too might have felt like me. How did you control this passion, Andreas?*

A24)   I didn't want to share it because it seemed so precious to me. Besides that I was scared that someone else would use my seeking against me. So weird ...

Q25)   *What is oneness?*

A25)   It is this. That which appears. The room, chairs, you, me, the conversation. That is oneness. And that is all there is.

Q26)   *Yet I can't know it.*

A26)   No, you can't. Oneness is not a thing. People, chairs,   you and me are not things. That is the dream: that there are lots of separate things going on. But there aren't any things. So, oneness is not many. And it is not one either. It is no-thing.

Q27) *Can I include various gods and goddesses, angels of various religions too in the list 'THERE ARE LOTS OF SEPARATE THINGS GOING ON'. ? Do you have anything else to say about the gods? Are they real or human imagination?*

A27) Nothing is real. Nothing is an object. Nothing is a thing. In that sense, the question about what Gods (really) are, remains unanswered.

Q28) *What you say is TOO GOOD to take. Nonetheless, I could see that 'WHAT IS' could only be as you say. You also say that what you talk is nothing new, and it has been spoken by many in the long past of human history. For instance, you quote, Master Eckhart. You are more explicit than Master Eckhart too. Well. You have obviously told me no help or guidance. Great. Do something as you are already accomplishing. All I can do is just cling to you as a baby monkey to its mother. Is this analogy ok with you?*

A28) Yeah, apparently this (non-)message has been spoken before, however, what's kind of new is its utter directness. Apparently, nowadays, it stands for itself without being embedded into any form of spirituality and/or tradition. Well, no baby, no mother! Though it looks and sounds very sweet ...

Q29) *"There is no step from presence to absence as this experienced presence is illusory already. Nothing is going to*

happen. Nothing is happening already." - Andreas.
If someone had told me this news, when I was 23 years old, when I started my spiritual search, now in my 70s, I would have avoided lot of conflicts and traumas in my life. Why it didn't happen? Who runs this cruel drama? And also, if I wish to tell this truth to a young person, to save him from peril, I find almost none is even interested to listen to this. Why this situation?

A29)   Oh well. No one runs this drama. It is what apparently happens - undone and for no reason at all.

Q30)   *Here is a personal problem. I've one comfortable/uncomfortable issue – alcohol.*
Fortunately, I'm not an alcoholic, or binge. For long stretch, I was a teetotaller too. Out of frustration with traditional spirituality, I relapsed to alcohol, and lo and behold! It mysteriously took me to Andreas Muller, who is my lifesaver now.
My little affinity with alcohol helps invigorating and fastly insightful too. But the crashing and hangover are utterly unpleasant. The sober hour seems a million times splendorous. How you westerners bypass this dilemma without making it an issue, Andreas? There are many books for that...not of much use...An enlightened being like you...

A30)   It is lovely to read from you. I, too, haven't found an answer to this problem yet. To not drink too much sounds like a good one, however, it can also be quite fun to drink. Maybe an idea is to not drink regularly ... one more of those ideas. You see, I have no clue ... .

Q31) Is Andreas is a) Vegetarian, b) Non-vegetarian, c) Vegan, d) All ?

A31) Andreas is d.), I guess.

Q32) "The assumption that there is a dream already is the dream. Dream is a dualistic concept" - Andreas
I can not understand this. It is the teachers who bring about this concept of dream. Normal people have no idea of dream even.

A32) Well, yes and no. "Normal people" have an idea of an "I" and the idea that something needs to happen. However, there is no 'I' that has to overcome anything.

Q33) "Nothing gets born and nothing dies. Both, so to speak, are simply no-thing as that. Yet, and that's important, for no one." - Andreas
As per the above message, suicide is simply a non event. Is it right?

A33) Yes, it is a non-event (like everything else).

Q34) What place has the concept of 'KARMA' in Andreas' message?

A34) There is no karma as such.

Q35) *'No-thing' has totally, absolutely, blossomed in Andreas.*
Does it make him sometimes get overwhelmed or excited, or
uncomfortable and make him go berserk for a while? May
be this phenomenon can happen to one in a billion human
being. Every now then, is there any strain sometimes in his
physical and mental energetic set up? Or does it simply feel
just ordinary? Traditional spirituality would either have
glorified such phenomenon as absolutely supernatural or
desecrated into blasphemy, isn't it?

A35) It is a bit hard to answer your question. There may be   all
kind of feelings, however, there isn't anyone who feels
overwhelmed by them. They just are what seems to be
happening.
What seems to be happening doesn't not feel in a
certain way.
Yes, you are totally right: Seen from the person,
apparent liberation is regarded as another personal
event that has to be "dealt" with.

Q36) *"All I say is empty. You can't get anything out of it"* -
Andreas
Good warning. Sounds harsh. Is there not a milder way to
convey this, sir?

A36) No, there isn't.

Q37)	"There is no 'me', no soul, no presence, no self- awareness and no self-consciousness". - Andreas
What way it is different from Nihilism?

A37)	Nihilism would be a concept or belief system that denies in order to give an answer or promote another standpoint. This message does not deny the me, it just points out apparently that there is no such thing.

Q38)	"There is nothing to know, because there is NO REALITY that can be known." - Andreas. Then what else is there?

A38)	There is not anything.

Q39)	"The miracle is that 'what is' is naturally whole and complete" - Andreas
How do you know that it is WHOLE and COMPLETE?

A39)	Yeah, that's a tough one - it cannot be known that what happens is whole and complete. Everything is whole and complete by simply being itself, however, there is no experience of wholeness.

Q40)	"No one is doing it, no one is observing it and no one is controlling it. THERE IS NO ONE". - Andreas
Then how there seems to be an 'order' in this chaos?

A40)   For no reason at all.

Q41)   *"There is neither a 'YOU', nor a 'REALITY', that can be experienced. There are no circumstances to arrive in. In that sense, it's WONDERFULLY HOPELESS". - Andreas*
Why don't you say, PATHETICALLY HOPELESS?

A41)   Because "hope" is part of the illusion that there is a person.

Q42)   *"There is no one left doing or not doing anything".*
- Andreas
Who says this?

A42)   No one - a blind report from no-thing.

Q43)   *Can we say, it is 'LOVE' that gives some meaning to this apparently absurd meaningless existence?*

A43)   Which existence do you refer to? There is no such thing,

Q44)   *Is there anything like resembling 'memory' that can exist in 'NO-THING'?*

A44)   I don't know what you mean.

Q45)   *"What is' is blindly itself. It has neither a clue about what it is nor if it even is". - Andreas*
WHO says this?

A45)   No one - a blind report from no-thing.

Q46)   *"There is no one" - Andreas*
Then why and how we as humans all have to unavoidably muddle with one another?

A46)   The muddling happens by itself, respectively is itself. There is just no 'I' doing that.

Q47)   *Karl Renz told us for time pass he watches TV or play video game called 'shooting ducks'. What does Andreas do?*

A47)   Reads the newspaper, goes for walks, watches YouTube, meets friends ...

Q48)   *"Even if there seems to be Andreas who wants this or that, there is no person behind it." - Andreas*
This truth applies to all x, y, & z. All apparently knows himself as a person. How humanity missed the vital fact that there is 'no person' at all behind it?

A48) Yes, there is no one. In a weird way, one could say that it is missed because there is no one to get it. Only when it drops, it drops.

Q49) *I want to be of some help to at least one person before I go. Your message seems to say none can be of any help to anyone. This is very pessimistic. Is it really so?*

A49) Yes, it is so. There is no 'I' which can be of help for another 'I'. That's all.

Q50) *What is - is it beingness or doesn't even know it exists ?*

A50) Yes, it does not know that it exists. "Beingness" is often confused with an experience of beingness. And there is no such thing.

Q51) *According to Andreas, what are the shortcomings of Spirituality?*

A51) It is a bit hard to talk about "shortcomings". There is nothing wrong with spirituality. The only thing I'd say is that it is based on an illusion: Namely that there is a spirit - a spiritual entity - in the first place. All spirituality is based on this assumption.

Q52) Let's say a person called Kumar who is enjoying in his   own ignorant world with unlimited money, drugs,sex,materials. Another side Andreas in his apparent world where he is living in moment by moment without any thinking mind, relaxing in the nondual nothingness. What's the difference? What's the advantage of Andreas over Kumar? According to Andreas point Kumar is also nothing ... From Kumar's point Andreas is a poor man with no sensory enjoyments. When both the bodies die after a certain time: What's going happen if both dissolve in nothingness? Why one needs to learn or talk about nothingness?

A52) There is no difference. There's just an apparent body Kumar living its life and an apparent body Andreas living its life.

Q53) Why this 5 sensory pleasures feels more likeable and desirable than the peace from self. If the sensory pleasures happening in self also must feel more orgasmic as in sex. Why it's not that way?

A53) There is no peace from self. There simply is no self.

Q54) If someone had told this fact to me, in my thirties or even forties, I would have avoided lot of traumas that I suffer in my seventies due to wrong spiritual training. OK, Better late than never. I've to slowly lick my wounds! There's no other faster way, though I've heard the truth through you.

A54) Oh yes, your life just was what seemed to have happened. There was no one in it. Never.

Q55) *If this is too personal you need not reply. Do you speak and relate with your life partner in the same way you communicate with us, your followers, or have a different style of communicating that is unique up to and only according to her ability of understanding your apparent self called Andreas? This question comes because, at least I can't be straight forward with my wife and our day today life challenges with my radical understanding of the message of Andreas, out of my love for her to be considerate with her ability to meet life and it's varieties of daily life challenges at least to avoid her deep disappointment with me.*

A55) Usually, I communicate very ordinarily. Non-duality is not an issue then and actually never brought on the table. There is no need to teach anyone, however, I understand that it can be quite difficult when there is no openness to this message or to what this message talks about.

Q56) *Do you take care of your body?*

A56) The body takes care of itself – as good or as bad as it is happening. I am quite okay so far.

Q57) *Is it not outrageous to make such statements:*

"'What is' doesn't experience itself as something that is."
"So-called existence is blind to itself."
"It just is. And is not."
How can something be - is, and is not? What makes you talk like this? Why it makes you talk like this?

A57)   Apparent Andreas talking like this is what seems to be happening. For no real reason, I guess.

Q58)   *"No-thing appearing to be deep sleep, no-thing appearing to be night dreaming and no-thing appearing to be sitting in a room. They are all timelessly no-thing. They simply don't exist...." - ANDREAS*
Andreas, Justine and others too don't exist? Or 'exist and don't exist' ? Or 'there is no one' to know? Or hard to answer? Or there is no answer? Or we will never know? Or ALL THE ABOVE?

A58)   Oh yes, in the end there is no answer to this. There is no answer, because there is no one to answer it.

Q59)   *My close friend physically died last month. Is he aware of himself as dead, as I am aware of myself being alive?*

A59)   Oh, no. There is no real awareness at all. The awareness to be alive is illusory.

Q60) *"There may be some who are around that message for a while, but the ones who aren't really ready – and I don't mean "ready" in a negative way or in terms of there being a path – lose interest very soon. They simply don't get what they are looking for. Their apparent needs just aren't recognized by me. They don't get the attention they long for. They don't get the entertainment they look for. They don't get highs of spiritual uplifting and so on. So, they go away after a while."- ANDREAS*
In that case, will they continue getting reborn in bodies, till they attain Moksha by sadhana?

A60) Well, apparently, the illusion that there is someone will be reborn every morning until the body drops. There is no difference between living as a "me" itself and doing sadhana. The "me" is seeking no matter which form it takes. In that sense: seeking = living = sadhana. Apparently, until this illusion becomes obvious as what it is: An apparent illusion.

Q60a) *Or Existence will discard and extinguish them when they are no more needed for its work, whether they try for freedom or not?*

A60a) There is no such thing as existence.

Q61) *What you talk about seems to be very complicated. I don't understand anything.*

A61) Actually, it's not complicated at all. There is nothing to understand. Seen by the apparent me, it all looks very complicated because that's exactly the world it assumes itself to live in: a real, complicated world that's made out of numerous parts, processes, interconnections, realities; in short: things that can – at least potentially – be known and understood. "I have to think about that and remember this and must not forget that" and so on. All of that doesn't exist.

Q62) *ALL OF THAT DOESN'T EXIST? Very pleasant to read. But... in this practical daily life - ALL OF THAT 'REALLY' DOESN'T EXIST ? Thanks for your time to reply my questions, Andreas*

A62) Oh yes, so-called practical life is what seems to be happening. It is not real in a sense that it happens to someone and there is someone doing any of that (so-called practical life). However, this is not answer for the person in order make its experience of practical life more comfortable. There is no one.

Q63) *Ramana said that knowing it is being it. How?*

A63) You CAN'T KNOW or rather EXPERIENCE it. You naturally are 'it'.´Yet, the seeker will probably turn this "being it" into something that one could or should consciously do. "Being it" is the natural reality, or rather: Everything already is that. For the seeker "being it" would mean to "become and experience to be it". But that's apparently different from being it. Yes, YOU ARE IT, but WITHOUT HAVING AN EXPERIENCE OF BEING IT.

Q64) *But how can it feel so real to be 'ME'?*

A64) If feeling to be 'ME' is what apparently happens over there, it's inevitable. Then that's what apparently happens, and that is reality, we could say. There is still NO ONE THERE though.

Q65) *But how can I comprehend that? How can I see that I'm not real?*

A65) Not at all. You can neither comprehend nor see that, just because 'THERE IS NO YOU'. Who would be able to do that? THERE IS NO ONE.

Q66) *Still we miss it. What can we do to clear the cluster? Don't say, no way.*

A66) There's no one to miss it. That's why there is no way ...

Q67) *Please don't take this as an insult. Were you diagnosed for autism, Asperger's syndrome, obsessive-compulsive disorder, or any other psychological issues?*

A67) No, I have never been diagnosed with any of these issues. And I don't think that I have any deep psychological issues (except "normal" psychological issues).

Q68) *It all feels very bitter, uncomfortable, useless. How you managed this? What or which helped?*

A68) Oh yes, this is un-managable. Nothing helps, but fortunately, there is no one.

Q69) *I think, my questions are going beyond limits. Are they all already answered?*

A69) Yes, No question, no answer ...

Q70) *Whatever you speak instantly brings in a BRIGHT SPOT. That's Freedom Itself. But there is a mind and body clamouring for some activity. Sure to put one into lot of trouble and unease. What to do?*
a) Let loose yourself into action
b) What has to happen will happen
c) One has no control on anything
d)After all there is no one to care or worry

e) Andreas has something peculiar to say on this.

A70)   Yes, I'd say: a), b), c) and d). E) I don't know about. I can't say if what I say is peculiar or not.

Q71)   *Do you have natural sleep of 8 hours every day?*

A71)   Yes, 6 - 8 hours.

Q72)   *How many hours of sleep is enough for you?*

A72)   I can function with 6.

Q73)   *Do you use pills like Xanax to sleep?*

A73)   Not at all.

Q74)   *Do you use daytime energy boosters?*

A74)   No.

Q75)   *How many cups of coffee do you consume per day?*

A75) Two - three. Sometimes one or none.

Q76) *Are you fond of Coca Cola?*

A76) Not really. However, sometimes I have one.

Q77) *Is your blood pressure normal?*

A77) I hope so.

Q78) *Do you find certain foods allergic or harmful?*

A78) Kiwi.

Q79) *Thank you very much for your clarity. I, too, want to become that clear. How?*

A79) It's an apparent clarity. I don't have anything from it. It doesn't serve me. I'm not referring to something that   still has to be realized and brought into existence. What I refer to is what's already happening. The clarity is apparent as there is nothing to be clear about. In that sense, it's utterly useless. I can't use it. Apparently, I still am as I am – as human, as touchable, as whatever I apparently am. This – 'what is' – doesn't need clarity. In fact, it's not real."

Q80) *"THIS - 'WHAT IS' - DOESN'T NEED CLARITY. IN FACT, IT'S NOT REAL." - Andreas*
If 'What is' is not real, then what is real?

A80) There is not something that's called 'what is'. All there is is what seems to be happening. It is nothing appearing to be whatever there seems to be. The apparent appearance of a tree cannot be clear about itself. It is just the apparent appearance of a tree.

Q81) *What is your opinion on hallucinogens?*

A81) I don't have an opinion on hallucinogens. They are what seems to be happening, but neither them nor their apparent effects mean something.

Q82) *How do you contain the bliss of 'WHAT IS'?*

A82) There isn't really "the bliss of 'WHAT IS'". There's simply what seems to be happening which cannot be contained. There's no container ...

Q83) *Do you believe in channelling on spirits?*

A83) Well, believe/not believe - I don't know. There may be   the apparent appearance of it.

Q84)   *What are your views on Astrology?*

A84)   I don't have any.

Q85)   *Why you never speak about the appalling misery and pain of living in a body on this earth?*

A85)   Well, the misery of being a 'me' is illusory. Everything   else is what seems to be happening and remains without answer.

Q86)   *Is it right to say: 'THE JOY IS - THERE'S NO ONE TO ENJOY'?*

A86)   Nothing is right or wrong to say. And yes, when there's joy that's what apparently happens to no one, respectively without a separate enjoyer.

Q87)   *Does Andreas feel connected to the events of the apparent world? Do they affect him?*

A87)   No, I do not feel connected. No separation does not mean that there is an experience of being unified. The events of the world are what seems to be happening and one's body is not separate from them. In that sense, there is constant affectation, however, there is no 'me' which is affected.

Q88) *You often use this message in your talks or writings: "But these things don't exist". Can you tell then, "WHAT DOES EXIST?".*

A88) No, I can't. There is nothing real to know anything in the first place. In that sense, the natural reality is a blind reality.

Q89) *Did you remember your past lives in different bodies during your drug experiments?*

A89) No, I didn't. At least, I wasn't aware of it back then. I had some insights in past lives, but only once within a so-called reincarnation/past live therapy. It was quite interesting at that time, but it didn't have a huge impact on me on general. I just did it once

Finals No. 1

Is spirituality too an illusion?

Oh yes, of course. Spirituality is based on the assumption that there is a spirit living in our bodies. All spirituality then circles around this assumed centre; usually working with attention, awareness and focus. However, it is this centre which is illusory and together with it, spirituality.

Is liberation waking up from one state to another?

No, it is not. Liberation is the sudden turning out that there are no states at all. In that sense, it is the collapse of the illusion that there is something which knows itself. In the end, there is no such thing as liberation.

Is there a Presence?

No, there is not.

What is right and what is wrong?

These two do not exist.

Is there an answer for our questions on existence?

No, there is not. It is this notion of existence which is dreamt - 'I am' or even 'am-ness' do not have any reality. So, all questions about existence only happen for an assumed something and are illusory.

What is this - 'What-is'?

There is no such thing as 'what is'. There is not anything.

What is the way out for us trapped in existence?

Well, no one is trapped.

What is the natural reality?

The term "the natural reality" does not refer to a specific way in which reality is. What seems to be happening just is purely itself - no matter if it is   thoughts, feelings, clouds, cars or deep sleep. They are naturally themself.

Is there a Reality?

No, there is not.

Are all our problems imagined ones?

Yes, there are no real problems. There is just life seemingly happening. The only illusion is that there is someone who needs to consciously "do" life. So-called problems are what seems to be happening.

'Me' is true or not?

There is no one.

'What is' too is an illusion?

No, what seems to be happening is not an illusion.

Bondage and liberation - are they not functional facts?

What seems to be happening is absolutely free to be what it is, however, it is also absolutely bound to be exactly as it is.

Delusion is a fact or not?

Which delusion?

Creation is true or not?

Which creation?

Who is the doer of things - man or God?

No one. There are no things.

Why there is always restlessness in us?

The sense to be present seems to be accompanied with a sense of unfulfilment and the need to move on.

How does a concrete world arise for us?

The impression of a substantial reality only happens for the illusion of beingness.

Is a guru essential to find freedom?

No.

Are pain and suffering too illusory?

It depends on what you regard as pain and suffering. Pain is what seems to be happening (if it happens). However, for no one. The sufferer is illusory.

Am I a dream too? Whose dream?

Yes, there is no 'I'. There is no dream.

Is 'I am' an illusion?

There is no 'I am'.

Seeking is a blessing or not?

Seeking is no-thing as that.

What comes and what goes?

Nothing comes, nothing goes, nothing is.

What is the advantage of effort?

There is no advantage of effort. Effort is illusory.

What wakes up in the morning - an illusion or truth?

Nothing wakes up in the morning. The impression to be something that wakes up in the morning, does not have any substance.

The sense of being separate is quite concrete and so real for everyone. Where is the element of dream in it?

It just is not real though it may seem like that.

Dreaming in sleep as dream is acceptable; but calling waking state as dream too is not acceptable, why?

I don't know.

Why 'awareness of something' is illusory?

For no reason. 'Awareness of something' never becomes existent, so all questions about it are coming from that illusory awareness.

Why liberation is death and not eternal life?

There is no such thing as life and death. There is no ongoing reality. In that sense, everything is timelessly itself.

Why there is no answer to anything?

Because there is not anything.

After all it is the person who attains liberation - why he/she is called an illusion?

There is no attainment of any kind. The person will never attain liberation or any special state. The person itself   is the illusion and all ideas of becoming are part of that illusion.

Is not 'no-thing' too a thing?

No, it is not.

How you say that in dying nothing happens?

> Because there is nothing happening in the first place. The idea of death happens for the one who experiences itself to be alive. However, this 'I am-ness' is illusory. When this melts away, nothing happens. It was never real in the first place.

To say for the 'me' this message is useless, is it not discouragement?

> The illusion to be someone is helplessly lost in being exactly this: An illusion. It is not just this message which is useless. Everything is useless. Nothing can be used by the apparent me to become a fulfilled me. Of course, this is discouraging, but only for an apparent illusion. The dream - and the prison - is the hope that something deeper can be found in this world. There is not anything.

Non-Duality says 'Nothing happens' - but everywhere something is always constantly happening. How to meet this riddle?

> The impression that something is happening belongs to the 'I'. Nothing else experiences 'happening'.

If 'What is' is blindly itself, how does it function with precision and exactness?

> It does not function. Reality is not an objectified reality which can or cannot function. All there is is an apparent appearance for no one.

How does the illusion of being 'me' happens?

There is no answer to that question, because actually, it does not happen. The illusion is that there is an illusion at all. Everything just is what seems to be happening.

What prompts to get rid of illusion?

Nothing.

How to drop the 'me' illusion?

There is no one.

There is no one - who says this?

No one. And there will never be anyone who can make this claim. Why? Because there is no one. The natural reality is a blind (= inexperienced) reality. There is no realization of "no one" and there never will be. So, don't wait. There is no one.

'Freedom - For no one', or the statement 'Oneness is for no one', may irritate the 'me', almost an insult for the 'me'. Can we find a softer way of saying it?

There is no one to protect.

If 'What is' is whole and complete, why or how do we miss it in our daily life?

Because there is no one. Apparent things being whole and complete can neither be seen nor missed. They just are that.

If 'What is' is uncreated, what is births and deaths in creation?

Birth and death are what is.

There is no bondage, no liberation, everything is beautifully itself. But what is the ugliness and cruelty around us?

Nothing.

What is illusion?

Nothing.

If apparent path cannot end the experience of separation, what else can? Grace?

There is no one.

If neither 'Who am I enquiry' nor 'there is no 'I' discovery ', can kill the 'I', what else can?

Nothing. "Killing the I" is an idea within the personal dream. Yet, there is no one.

Can we not create a procedure to get established in 'there is no I' and 'nothing to get'?

Oh no, of course, we can't. Who is this "we"? Who wants the realization of "no I"? Only "I" can want that. Only "I" seeks for salvation. It is this "I"which is without substance already.

There's no personal fulfilment because there's no person. How to drop the person? Surrender? Surrender to whom or what?

Who wants to drop the person? Who seeks for an answer, a way out? What lives in this beautiful arrogance and assumes that it can do "surrender"? This "me" is not real.

There is no teaching. Is it not this too a teaching?

Who could teach? Who could be taught? Why? This is all the dream.

Can a thing be simultaneously real and unreal?

Yes, however, then it is not a thing any more.

Any recognition is empty and meaningless. Even this conversation?

Yes, absolutely.

Is there a God?

No, there is not.

If there simply is no one there before waking up in the morning, who or what wakes up?

Nothing.

***

Finals No. 2

Your message sounds very much like Nihilism. Where does it differ from it?

Nihilism is a philosophy coming from a personal standpoint. Apparently, there is a "me" dismissing everything it becomes aware of. However, it cannot dismiss itself as an experienced reality. This message does not dismiss anything. It just points out the illusory nature of what seems to be happening and exposes the illusion of "am-ness" to be what it is: illusory.

Is time true?

There is nothing real.

The advaita teaching 'Be what you are' - does it work?

'Be what you are' may be an apparent description of what we talk about here, however, the desperate seeker turned it into a teaching. Everything being what it is is already the case.

Can 'awareness state' bring enduring peace?

It is the awareness state which is dreamt. There is no enduring peace.

If all is already whole, why we experience separation and conflict?

For no reason.

You say this room, my breathing, my feelings, this fan, all are well as they are. But why do we endlessly experience only craving, restlessness, and anxiety?

There is no one.

'Me' suffers illusory issues. Can this 'me' be dropped by will?

There is no "me" to drop.

If all is 'dreamt reality', who or what dreams?

The only dream is the personal experience; a dream that itself is not real.

'Being it' is natural reality. Experiencing it is suffering. Can we just 'be'?

No, we cannot. Everything is, but without the experience of beingness.

You say sitting in this chair, being me, being you, with thoughts and feelings is real for no one. Can we say, it's real only for the 'me'?

Yes, it seems real for the apparent "me". Yet, these things never are real.

No insights, no awareness, no arrival, no attainment - is it not exactly a zombie state?

No, it is not. The "me" is the zombie. Half alive, half dead, constantly greedy for fulfilment.

Is there no self awareness?

No, there is not.

Is there a state of 'deeper' Realisation?

No, there is not.

If 'What is' is COMPLETE, why do we feel incomplete and lacking?

For no reason.

Can we be aware of being aware?

'Being aware of being aware' is the person's dream of self-knowledge. It is this awareness which is unreal.

This is timelessly nothing. Apparent person is dream. Why this dream is not only unpleasant but cruel too?

For no reason.

Is there anything real?

No, there is not.

Can 'What is' be known?

There is no such thing as "what is".

Can one become realized?

There is not 'one'.

All seems dead and boring. Is happiness and bliss not possible here?

Totality is not boring. It just is impersonal.

Why there are no answers for questions?

> The seeker and its questions are illusory in the first place. There are no real questions to start with. They all refer to a reality that does not exist.

Any personal story is full of holes, but why we delight in it?

> Inventing a congruent story is a method of the person to confirm its existence. However, it is just a fantasy.

Is consciousness a real happening?

> No, it is not.

What is 'Maya'? Is there 'Maya'?

> No, there is not. The assumption that there is Maya is Maya.

Is creation true?

> No, it is not.

Can we not end the dream of existence?

> No, we can not, simply because there is no existence in the first place.

Why spirituality fails to deliver the promised goods?

> Because there is no spirit.

What does it mean: 'Be quiet'? Can one do that?

> Usually, it is referred to as a state of not-moving and/or not-thinking. Yet, there is no one.

Is there a way to find 'who am I'?

> No, there is not.

Can one know the 'Reality'?

> No, one cannot know reality. There is neither "one" nor "reality".

Is reincarnation true?

> First of all, there is no incarnation.

What is deep sleep?

> No-thing.

Can the traumas of life be dropped in a sweep?

> Maybe. If it is what seems to be happening.

Has Andreas message the highs of spirituality?

> This message is a great equalizer.

Does seeking solve problems?

No, it does not. It just perpetuates the illusion of personal problem solving.

'Well-being' is natural reality. What contaminates it for us to suffer?

The natural reality.

Is there anything to know?

No, there is not.

It is apparent that someone is doing something. How can you say that there is no one?

It only seems real when there is the illusion of   beingness. When this illusion drops, the impression of doer-ship (and observer) drops.

For us life means experiences. How do you say, experiencing does not exist?

It just does not. There is no "us".

If there is no real advantage or disadvantage in anything, what are we doing here? Where is meaning in all this?

There is no meaning in what seems to be happening. It is everything.

If nothing comes and ends what is this all about?

Nothing.

Ending up in the 'eternal' or in the 'always now' - is it not a supreme goal?

> The hope that there is a supreme goal is an idea that happens within the dream of "me". What seems to be happening is already everything.

Is it not wonderful to simply be here?

> There is no one who is being here. However, yes, there is no lack at all. 'What happens' is the wonder of no- thing.

What is liberation?

> Freedom.

Is not effort essential to stop the whirling around in the dream of person?

> No, it is not. The effort to stop whirling around within the dream is part of the dream.

Seen by the 'me', this message is absolutely useless – why?

> Because it can not be used.

It's whole and free. Why can't I see or abide in that?

> What happens being whole and complete is not everything. There is no 'I' within that.

I am in suffering and I want to get out. You say I can't. Is it not a merciless message?

There is no 'I'. This seems merciless, however, it just exposes the illusion of suffering as inexistent.

Sitting with gurus healed me a lot, though pain continues. Is it not outrageous to say gurus can't help?

There is no help in terms of "becoming a fulfilled me". There are no gurus, no disciples, no one who has lost fulfilment and no one who can find or become fulfilment.

It is called as "Empty fullness; but for no one". Isn't there someone?

No, there is not someone.

Is the 'I' who wants to surrender to God an illusion? Then how to attain salvation?

No 'I', no salvation.

If insights, conclusion and clarity are not answers, what else is?

There is no answer. Everything is timelessly itself.

Your statement "the sufferer is illusory; none suffer from anything" - is it not against the practical fact that all is suffering and sorrow?

All is sorrow? What an illusion!

Do we exist or not?

There is no one.

Why 'What-is' is unknowable?

> There is no 'what is' in the sense that there is an absolute reality. What seems to be happening is absolutely itself, however, it is not experienced by anyone. There is no experiencer outside of what seems 'to be happening. No experience equals no knowledge.

All that we have is a personal life - how can you say that there is no personal life?

> Because there is no person.

Why do you say, the idea of being someone on a path is a dream?

> Because there is no one.

If there is no success and no failure, what we humans are struggling for?

> Yes, there is no one who will and needs to become fulfilled.

Why seekers discard the simplicity of 'What-is' and muddle with themselves? Is 'what-is' that much complicated?

> Seekers are "what seems to be happening" as well. Effortlessly, freely, wholly.

Is there no way to find 'who am I'?

> No, there is not.

Really, is there anything to discuss?

No, there is not.

Why to stay in the 'I am' is futile?

Because there is no 'I am'.

You say 'nothing is free and nothing is imprisoned'. Then, how is it? It just is?

What seems to be happening is and is not.

It neither needs pointers nor needs any Realisation. Why do we crave for knowing?

No one is craving for knowing.

Personal teachings promise fulfilment. Why the seekers get utterly disappointed?

Because there is no such thing as a person.

Is there nothing to find?

Yes, there is nothing to find.

Why there is no way to realize oneness?

Because there is no one.

Is God absolutely blind?

There is nothing.

Why Reality cannot be reached by me?

Because there is no separation.

Why don't I find real fulfilment?

Because there is not anyone who is really unfulfilled.

WHAT REMAINS? - NOTHING.

There is nothing to realise, nothing to do and nothing not to do. There is no message.You cannot sum it up and get it all together, simply because there is nothing separate.

NO-THING appears as this. THAT IS IT. Nothing to be understood. Nothing to be realised. Nothing to be approached. It already is 'IT'. It already is whole - amazingly, as it is.

THAT IS THE MIRACLE, THE FREEDOM AND THE BEAUTY.

Disclaimer

The Authors of this E-Book 'Freedom for No One – Thoughts on Non-duality' shall not be responsible for the results of any actions arising out of the use of any information in this publication nor for any errors or omissions contained therein.
The Authors expressly disclaim all liability to any person in respect of anything and the consequences of anything done or omitted to be done by any such person in reliance, whether whole or partial upon the whole or any part of the contents.